Celebrating
Chinese
New Year

Fay Robinson

Enslow Elementary

an imprint of

Enslow Publishers, Inc.

E

40 Industrial Road
Box 398
Berkeley Heights, NJ 07922
USA

http://www.enslow.com

Enslow Elementary, an imprint of Enslow Publishers, Inc.

Enslow Elementary® is a registered trademark of Enslow Publishers, Inc.

Original edition published as *Chinese New Year* in 1996.

Library of Congress Cataloging-in-Publication Data

Robinson, Fay.
   Celebrating Chinese New Year / Fay Robinson.
     p. cm. — (Celebrating holidays)
     Summary: "Read about the dragon parade, the holiday's beginnings, symbols and beliefs, and
    celebrating the New Year"—Provided by publisher.
   Includes bibliographical references and index.
   ISBN 978-0-7660-4031-1 (alk. paper)
    1. Chinese New Year—United States—Juvenile literature. 2. United States—Social life and
    customs—Juvenile literature. I. Title.
GT4905.R625 2011
394.261—dc23   2011021329

Future Editions
Paperback ISBN 978-1-59845-398-0
ePUB ISBN 978-1-4645-1082-3
PDF ISBN 978-1-4646-1082-0

Printed in China.

012012 Leo Paper Group, Heshan City, Guangdong, China

10 9 8 7 6 5 4 3 2 1

To Our Readers:
We have done our best to make sure all Internet addresses in this book were active and appropriate
when we went to press. However, the author and the publisher have no control over and assume
no liability for the material available on those Internet sites or on other Web sites they may link to.
Any comments or suggestions can be sent by e-mail to comments@enslow.com or to the address
on the back cover.

CONTENTS

A man holds up a decorated dragon head to celebrate the New Year.

CHAPTER 1

THE DRAGON PARADE

It is evening, and it is also the end of the New Year's celebration in Chinatown in San Francisco, California. A large crowd has gathered on the streets. It is hard to find a place to stand. Thousands of people are watching and waiting for a parade.

As darkness arrives, a band marches past the crowds. The parade has begun! Floats that look like they are decorated with flowers roll by. Important people pass in cars with horns honking. Miss Chinatown USA waves to the crowd. She is standing high on a special float. Children in red silk clothes perform a Chinese dance.

LOTS OF PARADES

Many different kinds of performers are part of the celebration. This woman is dressed in costume. She is marching in a parade to celebrate the new year.

There are many different kinds of dragon heads carried through the Chinese New Year festival.

Athletes stop to do amazing tricks. More floats, more bands, and more performers come down the street. For more than two hours, the wonderful sights of the parade roll by.

With glittery scales and flashing eyes, a dragon weaves up the street. It is made of colorful cloth, and the people underneath it are holding up its body with poles. It twists and turns, and sways back and forth like a giant puppet. The dragon is supposed to bring good luck for the year to come.

Last, but not least, a long string of firecrackers starts to explode. For several minutes the sounds and sights of popping firecrackers fill the air. The firecrackers leave a trail of smoke as they explode.

The dragon parade marks the end of the New Year's celebration for Chinese Americans. But what is the rest of the holiday like, and why is this holiday so important?

The dragon parade is an important part of many Chinese New Year celebrations.

CHAPTER 2

THE HOLIDAY'S BEGINNINGS

Chinese New Year is a very old holiday. It started more than four thousand years ago in China. Now it is celebrated all around the world, in any place where large groups of Chinese people live. It does not always come on the same date each year, but it is always in January or February.

CELEBRATING THE NEW YEAR

There are similar celebrations in Japan, Korea, and Vietnam known as the Lunar New Year or the Spring Festival. In San Francisco, California, Chinese New Year is also called Lunar New Year.

A LION PARADE

Dancers who are dressed in this lion costume in China celebrate the new year. Chinese New Year started more than four thousand years ago in China. Today people from all over the world celebrate.

To understand why this holiday is celebrated the way it is, it helps to know a little about China. Farming has always been very important in China. It is still very important today. Long ago the harvesting and

Farming has always been important in China. Plants are an important part of celebrating the new year.

planting seasons were the most important times of the year. The harvest was a time to celebrate. It marked the end of another year. If the growing season was good, there would be plenty of food and everyone would be happy. The Chinese New Year holiday started as a way to celebrate the end of one planting season and the beginning of another.

People ate special foods and spent extra time with family and friends at this time. Then they marched through their villages carrying lanterns, special lamps, to chase away the old year. They hoped the lanterns would help bring out the light and warmth of spring. These celebrations ended with firecrackers, just as they do today. A folktale explains the importance of the firecrackers.

Lanterns are supposed to bring out the light and warmth of spring.

People eat special foods and spend extra time with family to celebrate the new year.

According to the story, a monster came down to the villages at this time of year to scare everyone. But one day, just by chance, people noticed that the monster was afraid of loud noises.

Bamboo is a type of tree, and the sticks that form the tree's trunk burst open with a bang when they burn. The air inside the hollow spaces of bamboo sticks expands—takes up more space—when it is heated by fire. The air keeps pushing on the bamboo sticks and—pop—they explode with a loud noise. These were the first firecrackers. Firecrackers have been used ever since to frighten away evil during Chinese New Year.

In Chinese, the word for firecracker means "exploding bamboo stick." Bamboo is the type of tree seen here.

Firecrackers

In China today, the word for firecracker is *baozhu*. It means "exploding bamboo stick." Bamboo is not used for firecrackers anymore. But, today firecrackers come in long, thin shapes just like small bamboo sticks.

The Chinese New Year is celebrated each year sometime between the middle of January and the middle of February. The exact date is different every year because this holiday is celebrated according to a Chinese lunar calendar. Each new month on the Chinese lunar calendar begins with a new moon. The Chinese New Year is celebrated on the first new moon of the year on the Chinese calendar.

China's Celebration

China is a very large country. It is much larger than the United States. In a country this big, there are many differences among the people, including how they celebrate holidays. Even today, Chinese New Year is celebrated differently in different parts of China. Chinese New Year is not exactly the same for every person in China, or for every Chinese American in the United States.

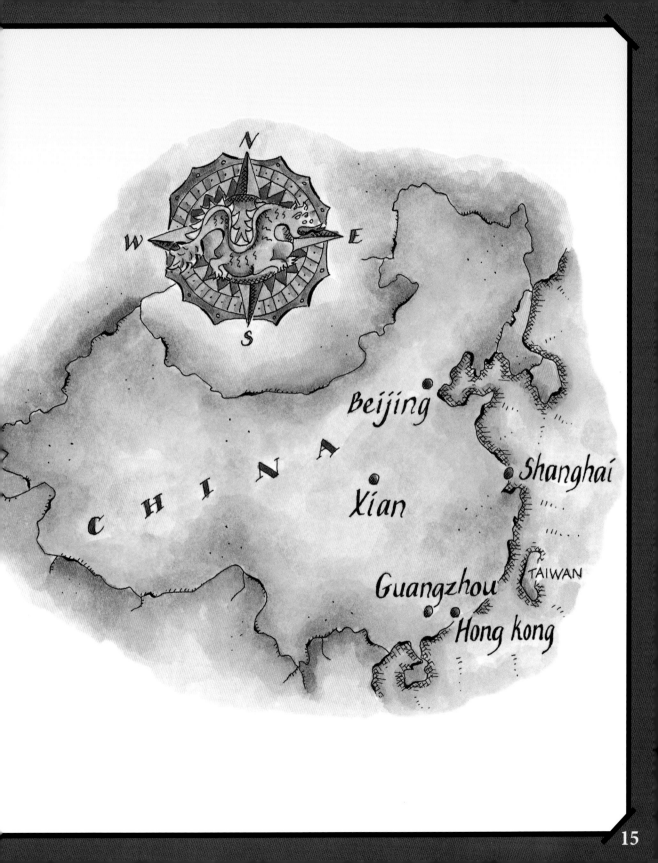

Look at the chart to see what animal
you are like:

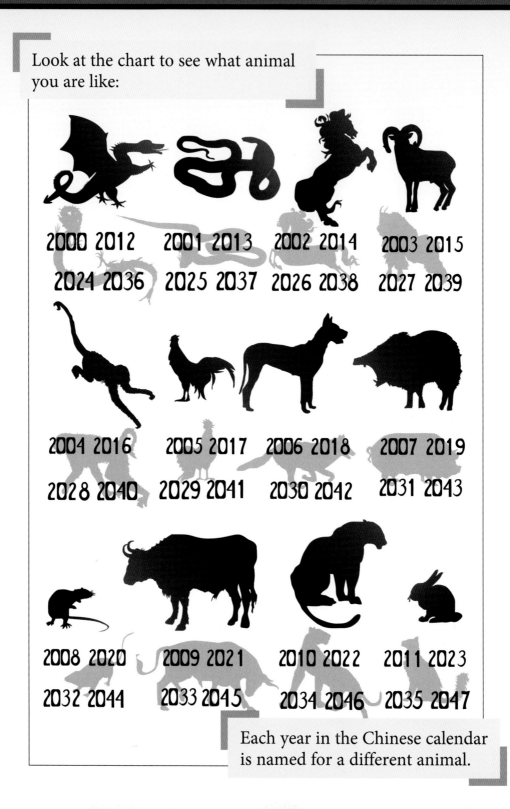

2000 2012   2001 2013   2002 2014   2003 2015
2024 2036   2025 2037   2026 2038   2027 2039

2004 2016   2005 2017   2006 2018   2007 2019
2028 2040   2029 2041   2030 2042   2031 2043

2008 2020   2009 2021   2010 2022   2011 2023
2032 2044   2033 2045   2034 2046   2035 2047

Each year in the Chinese calendar
is named for a different animal.

THE CHINESE CALENDAR

Every year in the Chinese calendar is named after an animal. The Chinese say that the year in which you were born tells what animal you are like. For example, if you were born in 2006, you were born in the year of the dog. Like a dog, you are loyal and trustworthy.

Here are some other animal descriptions:

Dragon: Strong, energetic and impressive

Rabbit: Tranquil, generous, and imaginative

Tiger: Competitive, optimistic, a leader

Ox: Honest, placid and considerate

Rat: Friendly, polite, and intelligent

Boar: Calm, tolerant, and optimistic

Dog: Alert, trustworthy, and faithful

Rooster: Frank, courageous, and good company

Monkey: Sociable, astute, and independent

Sheep: Gentle, amiable, and sensitive

Horse: Friendly, eloquent, and loyal

Snake: Elegant, refined, and confident

A traditional Chinese lantern is lit up during Chinese New Year.

CHAPTER 3

SYMBOLS AND BELIEFS

The Chinese people of long ago believed in many different gods. They also felt they could bring luck, wealth, and happiness into their lives by doing certain things. Many objects were symbols, things that stood for something else. The beliefs in gods and symbols are still part of Chinese New Year's traditions.

A HAPPY NEW YEAR

Red is the color of happiness. People may hang poems written on red paper to celebrate Chinese New Year.

CLEANING

It is important to clean and scrub the home before the new year arrives. Cleaning is started about a month before the new year and must be finished before the celebrations start.

The Chinese people of long ago believed in many different gods.

DECORATIONS

After the house is clean, some people put up special New Year's decorations. Red is the color of happiness. Two-line poems, written on red paper, may be hung side by side on the walls. They are filled with good wishes for the family. The Chinese word for luck can be placed around the house. By putting up these wishes, people hope good things will come to them.

LOOKING GOOD

People may get their hair cut before the new year. Everyone wants to start the new year looking their best. People do not want to have to get a haircut after the beginning of the new year. Cutting hair—or cutting anything—would be like cutting your luck. Some people also get new clothes to show that New Year's Day is a time for new beginnings.

FLOWERS

In the few days before the new year, some people buy flowers, such as narcissus, azaleas, and quince blossoms, to place around their homes and to give away as gifts. Flowers are symbols of growth. Some people believe that if a flower blooms on New Year's Day, it is a sign that the year ahead will be a good one.

Some people buy flowers like these narcissus blooms before the new year. Flowers are a symbol of growth.

Fruits such as oranges and tangerines stand for wealth and good fortune. They are often placed around the home.

FRUIT

Special bowls of fruit may be placed around the home. Oranges and tangerines stand for wealth and good fortune and are used most often. The Chinese word for them sounds like the word for good luck. Chinese people in the United States often use these same fruits for decoration. Pummelos, Chinese grapefruit, can also be used.

DEBTS

If anyone owes money to stores or friends, they must pay it back before New Year's Day. Long ago in China, storeowners came to people's doors to get money they were owed. If the people did not pay, storeowners hung a lantern outside the door. The lantern told everyone passing by that the family in that house owed money to someone. This was very embarrassing, so everyone tried hard to pay what they owed.

COOKING

Chinese New Year is a time for special foods. There is a great feast on New Year's Eve, the night before New Year's Day, and more big meals on the days that follow. Everything must be prepared before New Year's Day. No one wants to work on that day. Many people believe if they do work that day, they will have to work harder during the rest of the year. Nian goa, the new year's cake, is prepared. It is believed that the higher the cake rises, the better the year will be.

Cake is often served to celebrate the new year. It is believed that the higher the cake rises, the better the new year will be.

SPECIAL FOODS

Certain foods have special meanings during the Chinese New Year. Here are some of them:

- fried rice = getting along
- pork = wealth
- duck = happiness
- fish = long life and good fortune
- dumpling = happy family life

Many different types of foods are served during the Chinese New Year.

THE KITCHEN GOD

The kitchen god was an important ancient god. Legend says that once each year, right before the new year, it was the kitchen god's job to report the behavior of everyone in the house to his boss, the "Jade Emperor."

Kumquats

Today, as part of the celebration of the Chinese New Year, sweets are often exchanged so that the kitchen god's report will be sweet and flattering. While many people no longer believe in the kitchen god, almost everyone likes the sweets!

Coconuts

Litchis

People give each other sweets such as dried kumquats, coconuts and litchis during the Chinese New Year.

Streetscape in Chinatown, Los Angeles, California.

CHAPTER 4

LET THE NEW YEAR BEGIN!

Finally it is New Year's Eve, and the whole family gathers for a feast. It is a time for enjoying the meal, being with family and friends, and remembering loved ones.

After dinner the family plays games and tells stories until, at last, it is midnight. An ancient Chinese superstition says that parents encourage children to stay awake as long as possible. Legend says that the longer the children stay awake, the longer their parents will live.

In China the fireworks begin at midnight and

A NIGHT TO STAY AWAKE

It is an ancient Chinese custom for children to stay awake as long as possible on New Year's Eve. Legend says that the longer the children stay awake, the longer their parents will live.

keep going until the early hours of the morning, before starting again at daybreak. In many Chinatowns in the United States, stores turn on their lights as the sun is coming up to welcome the new year. Children wake up and greet their parents with New Year's wishes. People put on their new clothes.

Family members may give the children red envelopes, called *ya sui qian,* filled with money. The amount of money is usually an even number because odd numbers are thought of as unlucky. The envelopes symbolize the giving and receiving of luck.

The Chinese believe that on New Year's Day, everyone is one year older. In traditional

In some Chinatowns, fireworks start at midnight and go on until dawn.

China, the day you were born is not as important as the year in which you were born.

Children use their best manners in honor of the new year. No one says anything bad about anyone else. It is thought that how people act on the first day of the new year affects their luck for the rest of the year.

For the next three to five days, people may visit relatives and friends, bringing gifts and good wishes. They say, "*Gung hay fat choy.*" This New Year's greeting means "Wishing you good fortune and wealth."

On New Year's Day, family members may give children red envelopes filled with money. The envelope stands for the giving and receiving of luck.

Outside, in front of stores, people dressed as lions might perform the Lion Dance. The Lion Dance is believed to chase away harm. Two or more

Stores put up banners for Chinese New Year. This one is for the year of the horse.

people are needed to make the colorful lion costume come to life. The person inside the head pulls on straps to make the glittery eyes wink and the huge jaws open. The lion shakes his head up and down to the sound of clashing cymbals and loud drums. Other dancers move his body and tail, making him leap and thrash.

When the dance is almost over, storeowners light strings of firecrackers. Finally, the noise ends and everyone claps. The lion moves on to the next store, but the celebration is not over yet.

Drumbeats awaken the lion during the lion dance.

The Chinese dragon costume is always part of the celebration.

CHAPTER 5

CELEBRATING THE NEW YEAR

For many people the most exciting part of the celebration of Chinese New Year is the dragon parade. In China, and in many places in the United States where people celebrate Chinese New Year, the parade takes place on the first full moon of the new year. This is the first day of spring on the Chinese calendar. It is the fifteenth day of the new year.

Cities in the United States, such as New York, Chicago, and San Francisco, have parades of different sizes. They usually include music and dance and important people. Some parades also have people wearing masks and costumes, funny jugglers, and people on stilts. Lanterns are part of the tradition in China. Some parades in the United States include a lantern show.

PARADES!

Parades are held in many cities all over the United States to celebrate Chinese New Year.

Wherever the parade takes place, it always ends with a dragon. Dragons are an important part of many Chinese festivals, including Chinese New Year.

Some people hang very fancy lanterns.

In ancient China, dragons did not breathe fire. They were wise and caring. They guarded the wind, the rain, and the rivers. The dragon in the parade symbolizes the coming of spring rains and sunshine. It is said he brings good luck.

DRAGONS, DRAGONS EVERYWHERE

Many countries use dragons in their art, especially China, Korea, and Japan. It is easy to tell the difference between Chinese, Korean, and Japanese dragons. Just count the dragon's toes:

- Chinese dragons have five toes.
- Korean dragons have four toes.
- Japanese dragons have three toes.

The dragon in the parade is moved by people walking underneath it. Dragons are often one hundred feet long—that is longer than three school buses in a row. It takes as many as fifty people to make the dragon dance. They use poles to hold the dragon's body up, weaving the body back and forth as they walk up the street. The person at the dragon's head can pull straps and push buttons to make the dragon's eyes flash and blink and its mouth open wide. The dragon is made of bright, colorful cloth that sparkles.

The dragons used in parades are often one hundred feet long. That is longer than three school buses lined up in a row.

THE DRAGON TAKES SHAPE

Long, long ago, the people of China lived in different tribes. Each tribe had a different animal to symbolize its strengths. Later, when the tribes joined together, the people joined the parts of the animals. The animal parts made one creature—the dragon. It is said that the dragon has:

- eyes of a rabbit
- head of a camel
- horns of a deer
- ears of an ox
- body of a snake
- scales of a carp (fish)
- whiskers of a catfish
- claws of a hawk
- feet of a tiger

Chinese New Year's celebrations in the United States are slightly different from city to city. Here is how some cities celebrate:

The dragon is a symbol of strength.

NEW YORK

In New York there are special shows with items from China on display in the libraries and community centers. People demonstrate some of the Chinese arts, such as tea ceremonies and Chinese writing. Dancers and musicians perform. It is a time for Chinese-American children who where born in the United States to learn about China. There are also firecrackers and a dragon parade.

CHICAGO

In Chicago a banquet, an elegant meal, is held in a fancy hotel on New Year's Eve. Chinese Americans from all over the city can go. It is often very cold in Chicago at this time of year, so the crowds outside enjoy a shorter dragon parade. People can go to Chinatown's restaurants afterward to enjoy special Chinese dishes. The lion dancers stop at storefronts after the parade, giving people a chance to watch from inside or outside.

SAN FRANCISCO

San Francisco has one of the largest populations of Chinese Americans in the United States. Its New Year's celebration is called Lunar New Year. It includes many Asian-American groups who celebrate the holiday, including Korean Americans and Vietnamese Americans. In San Francisco,

The official entrance to Chinatown in San Francisco, California.

Lunar New Year is celebrated the traditional way, for fifteen days. The dragon parade in San Francisco is a huge event. It lasts for more than two hours. The dragon is more than two hundred feet long.

OTHER, SMALLER CITIES

Some towns and cities have very small numbers of Chinese Americans. So how do they celebrate this important holiday?

Groups of Chinese Americans may gather on New Year's Eve for the traditional meal. Friends who are not Chinese may be invited, too. People eat and enjoy one another's company for the evening. It is a very special dinner, even though it is a quiet celebration.

Today in China there is a large celebration that is shown on television. People in the United States who get China's television station can watch this celebration. Often

As part of the New Year's Eve celebration, people eat and enjoy each other's company.

The sky over Victoria Harbor bursts into a colorful display to celebrate the Lunar New Year in Hong Kong.

Chinese-American families and friends watch together. This helps them to feel the spirit of their home country even though they are far away. Sometimes Chinese Americans with relatives in China will call each other on the telephone as they watch. That way they can share the excitement.

No matter how this holiday is celebrated, there are some things all Chinese New Year's celebrations have in common. Good food, lions, a dragon parade, firecrackers, and, most important, spending time with family and friends, are all part of this holiday. This is a warm, happy holiday full of good wishes. Happy New Year! Gung hay fat choy! Wishing you good fortune and wealth!

Chinese New Year is a time for lions, dragon parades, and spending time with family.

Chinese New Year Craft Project

Make Ya Sui Qian—Money Envelopes

You can make ya sui qian, red envelopes for gifts of money. You will need:

- pencil
- shiny red paper
- safety scissors
- glue
- pretend money
- tape

1 Trace or copy the shape formed by the solid lines below onto the red paper.

2 Draw in the dotted lines on your red paper. Cut along the solid lines.

3 Fold the flaps in toward the dotted lines in order by number, starting with one. Glue them in place. Allow the glue to dry.

4 Place pretend money in the envelope.

5 Fold the top flap down and tape it in place.

6 Give your ya sui qian to someone special for Chinese New Year. Be sure to say "gung hay fat choy!"

*Safety Note: Be sure to ask for help from an adult, if needed, to complete this project.

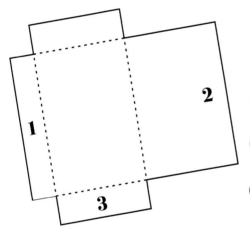

Words to Know

celebrate—To take part in a joyful time.

Chinatown—A neighborhood in some cities in the United States, such as New York, Chicago, and San Francisco, where many Chinese Americans choose to live.

firecrackers—Stick-shaped rods that explode with a bang when they are lit.

float—A moving display in a parade.

Gung hay fat choy—A Chinese New Year's greeting that means "wishing you good fortune and wealth."

symbol—Something that stands for something else.

tradition—A way of doing something that is passed on over time.

ya sui qian—Chinese New Year's gifts of red envelopes with money inside them.

Read More About

Chin, Oliver. *The Year of the Rabbit: Tales from the Chinese Zodiac*. San Francisco, California: Immedium, 2010.

Jango-Cohen, Judith. *Chinese New Year*. Minneapolis, Minnesota: Carolrhoda Books, Inc., 2005.

Otto, Carolyn. *Holidays Around the World: Celebrate Chinese New Year: With Fireworks, Dragons, and Lanterns*. Washington, D.C.: National Geographic Children's Books, 2009.

Internet Addresses

"CHINA THE BEAUTIFUL"
<http://www.chinapage.com/newyear.html>
This website directs you to interesting and informative facts about the Chinese calendar.

"KABOOSE"
<http://crafts.kaboose.com/holidays/chinese_new_year .html>
You will find that this website offers Chinese New Year fun facts, recipes and crafts!

"APPLES4THETEACHER"
<http://www.apples4theteacher.com>
A wonderful educational website which offers teachers and kids educational games, crafts, activities and more!

Index